CONTENTS

CATWOMAN
GOTHAM CITY'S NUMBER ONE CAT BURGLAR

VITAL STATS

LIKES: Diamonds
DISLIKES: Getting caught
FRIENDS: Batman
FOES: Batman
SKILLS: Quick getaways
GEAR: Whip

SET NAMES: Catwoman Catcycle City Chase
SET NUMBERS: 6858
YEARS: 2012

DID YOU KNOW?
Catwoman appears in all three of the LEGO® Batman™ video games, along with her cat, Isis.

Mask doubles as a Catcycle helmet

White goggles keep Catwoman's eyes hidden

Catwoman's 2012 costume comes complete with a chunkier zip and belt.

LITTLE BLACK CATSUIT

Catwoman's 2006 minifigure wears a stealthy black catsuit with a matching black mask and simpler torso detailing. Armed with her trusty whip, this cat burglar is ready to tangle with Batman in The Batman Dragster: Catwoman Pursuit (set 7779).

Glamorous Selina Kyle has a weakness for glittering diamonds. No gem is safe while Catwoman is on the prowl. A talented gymnast, Selina often has to make acrobatic escapes from Batman.

CATCYCLE
MEEEEEOWWWWW!

VITAL STATS

OWNER: Catwoman
USED FOR: Cat burglary
GEAR: Whip

SET NAME: Catwoman
Catcycle City Chase
SET NUMBER: 6858
YEAR: 2012

Stolen diamond

In-built grip for a whip

Kickstand in raised position

EYES ON THE ROAD
The Catcycle in The Batman Dragster: Catwoman Pursuit (set 7779) has cat's eyes and ears at the front and an exhaust flame trailing like a cat's tail.

Speeding like a cheetah, Selina Kyle's catlike bike can whisk her from crime scene to crime scene with barely a pause. Her two wheels purr along nicely – whether she's driving to commit the crimes or solve them.

KILLER CROC
COLD-BLOODED CROOK

LIKES: Wrestling alligators
DISLIKES: People making fun of his appearance
FRIENDS: The Penguin
FOES: Batman and Robin
SKILLS: Fast healing
GEAR: Gun

SET NAMES: The Batboat: Hunt for Killer Croc
SET NUMBERS: 7780
YEARS: 2006

Exclusive scaly face printing

Narrowed red eyes

Scales continue on unique torso printing

SCALE MODEL
Killer Croc does his best to outpace the Batboat in this small speedboat. Part of the character's only LEGO set appearance to date, it features exclusive crocodile-face printing and swamp-green missiles.

With a grin to rival the Joker's, this reptilian rascal could snap at any moment! He may not have much in the way of brains, but his tough, scaly skin and super-strength make him the mean, green king of Gotham City's swamps.

TWO-FACE
DON'T GET ON HIS BAD SIDE!

VITAL STATS
....

LIKES: Playing heads or tails
DISLIKES: Matching outfits
FRIENDS: His other half
FOES: Batman
SKILLS: Seeing things from both sides
GEAR: Machine gun, lucky coin

SET NAMES: The Batmobile: Two-Face's Escape
SET NUMBERS: 7781
YEARS: 2006

Unruly hair on left-hand side of head

Purple facial scarring only covers left-hand side of face

White suit on dark-haired side... and dark suit on white-haired side!

SPLITTING HAIRS

Two-Face was the first LEGO minifigure to have multicoloured hair – made from white plastic with black printing. Poison Ivy and Wonder Woman also have printing on their hair pieces.

Lots of people in Gotham City lead double lives, but Two-Face takes it to extremes! One of the city's biggest crime bosses, he is in two minds about everything and makes decisions by flipping his lucky coin – unlucky for some!

TWO-FACE'S HENCHMAN
BANDED BANDIT

Black and white
jersey echoes
Two-Face's suit

Black
handgun

HEELS ON WHEELS
The bank truck hijacked by
Two-Face and his Henchman
boasts an armoured windshield,
a booby-trapped roof and hidden
weapons that fold out from the
sides of the vehicle.

What's black and white and green
all over? A stolen Gotham City Bank
truck filled with banknotes and
Two-Face's goon! This Henchman
is always happy to help out with
a bank heist – though you wouldn't
know it from the look on his face!

THE JOKER
THE CLOWN PRINCE OF CRIME

Unique green
hair piece with
pointed edges

Laughter lines
around eyes and
mouth from too
much grinning

Don't sniff the flower
– it spits acid!

FUN IN THE GUN
The Joker's armoury of
outlandish weapons ranges
from the silly to the scary. One
of his favourites is a gun that
fires a flag with the word
"BANG!" written on it.

This clownish character is no
fool: he's the prince of crime in
Gotham City! His grin hides a deep
hatred of Batman and Robin, and
his jokes always have a sting in the
tail. He is out to cause chaos at
every comic turn!

THE JOKER'S HENCHMAN
WILL WORK FOR SNACKS

VITAL STATS
....

LIKES: Ice lollies
DISLIKES: Brain freeze
FRIENDS: The Joker,
Mr Freeze
FOES: Batman and Robin
SKILLS: Flying the Joker's
helicopter
GEAR: Nice hat

SET NAMES: The Batwing:
The Joker's Aerial Assault,
The Tumbler: Joker's Ice
Cream Surprise
SET NUMBERS: 7782, 7888
YEARS: 2006, 2008

Classic henchman hat

Purple top matches
the Joker's jacket

Ice lolly from the
Joker's Ice-Cream Van

IT'S THAT MAN AGAIN
A familiar-looking Henchman
also assists Mr Freeze in The
Batcave: The Penguin and Mr
Freeze's Invasion (set 7783).
He wears a blue top and black
gloves along with his usual hat.

The Joker's Henchman looks
remarkably like Two-Face's
Henchman. Perhaps he is the same
hired hand, prepared to do the
dirty work for whoever keeps him
stocked up with sunglasses and
knitted hats – or ice lollies!

THE JOKER COPTER
SKY-HIGH SURPRISE

The Joker's Henchman is at the controls!

VITAL STATS
....

OWNED BY: The Joker
USED FOR: Dropping laughing gas on Gotham
GEAR: Missiles, gas bombs

SET NAMES: The Batwing: The Joker's Aerial Assault
SET NUMBERS: 7782
YEARS: 2006

Copter sides fold down to reveal missiles

BOMBS AWAY
Pulling the rod at the back of the Copter releases grinning green gas bombs from a hidden compartment. The Joker also likes to throw these while hanging from the rope ladder!

Detachable rope ladder held in place with LEGO® Technic pin

This helicopter looks harmless – until its sides fold down to reveal hidden weapons! Part of the Joker's plan to cover Gotham City with toxic laughing gas, it can also use its side-mounted satellite dish to deflect missiles from Batman's Batwing.

THE JOKER'S ICE CREAM TRUCK
THE CHILLING JOKE

VITAL STATS

OWNED BY: The Joker
USED FOR: Selling Joker-gas ice creams
GEAR: Missile launcher

SET NAMES: The Tumbler: Joker's Ice Cream Surprise
SET NUMBERS: 7888
YEARS: 2008

Missile launcher disguised within giant multi-coloured ice-cream scoops

Logo promises a surprise – but not a nice one!

Spring-loaded missile

NOT-SO-NICE CREAM

Three very unpleasant sounding flavours of ice cream are listed on the back of the Joker's truck: Soda Smile Pop Sickle, Ol' Fashioned Venom Flavour, and Rigor Mortis Soft Ice!

Venom for making toxic ice creams goes inside slots labelled "venom"

Registration plate reads "I Scream"

The colourful cone on top of this truck isn't just for show – it's also a lever that fires a giant missile out through the back doors! The Joker will need this secret weapon when Batman hears about his tasteless plan to sell toxic gas ice creams.

THE PENGUIN
FREE AS A BIRD

VITAL STATS

LIKES: Sharp tailoring
DISLIKES: Prison jumpsuits
FRIENDS: The Arkham Asylum inmates
FOES: Batman and Robin
SKILLS: Operating riotous rides
GEAR: Umbrella, fish, gun

SET NAMES: Batman: Arkham Asylum Breakout, Jokerland
SET NUMBERS: 10937, 76035
YEARS: 2013, 2015

DID YOU KNOW?
The original 2006 Penguin minifigure didn't have an eye showing through his monocle.

Monocle

Umbrella doubles as a weapon

Purple mini-legs

DRESSED TO IMPRESS
Batman's oldest foe, the Penguin fancies himself as an upstanding Gotham City citizen. Always impeccably dressed, the original 2006 Penguin minifigure wore an elegant tuxedo with an orange waistcoat in sets 7783 and 7885.

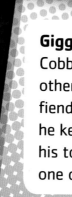

Giggling gangster Oswald Cobblepot loves waddling off with other people's riches. The fowl fiend is no featherbrain, although he keeps his secrets safely under his top hat, and is never far from one of his gadget-laden umbrellas.

THE PENGUIN SUBMARINE
SWIMMING WITH THE FISHES

VITAL STATS
....

OWNER: The Penguin
USED FOR: Jewel theft
GEAR: Missiles fore and aft

SET NAME: Robin's Scuba Jet: Attack of The Penguin
SET NUMBER: 7885
YEAR: 2008

Periscope for seeing what's going on above water

Torpedo launcher

Tower section lifts off

Intimidating Penguin face on prow

GOING UNDERGROUND
With Mr Freeze on board, the Penguin sets course for Batman's secret base in The Batcave: The Penguin and Mr Freeze's Invasion (set 7783). This earlier sub is labelled U98 on the side.

Lever fires a missile from the stern

The Penguin's tally of Bat battles!

Numbered U99 (the "U" stands for "undersea"), this sub swims as well as a real seabird! On the hull, the Penguin has marked the fact that he has fought four battles with Batman, and is now hoping to get away with a stolen crystal!

MR. FREEZE
COLD-HEARTED SCIENTIST

Goggles worn over
eyes that are capable
of producing icy blasts

Helmet keeps this
criminal cool

STONE COLD STEAL

Mr Freeze wields a different ray
gun as he makes his getaway
from a diamond robbery. Driving
a sub-zero speedster, he hopes
to freeze Batman's pursuing
Buggy in its tracks!

Freeze ray puts
enemies on ice

Backpack
pumps coolant
around suit

A lab accident permanently lowered
Dr. Victor Fries' body temperature,
forcing him to wear a special suit
of armour at all times. Now calling
himself Mr Freeze, he turned to
crime to fund his scientific research.

POISON IVY
NAUGHTY BY NATURE

VITAL STATS

LIKES: Plants and flowers
DISLIKES: Pesticides
FRIENDS: Bane
FOES: Batman and Robin
SKILLS: Biology, plant control
GEAR: Twisted vines

SET NAMES: The Batcave, Batman: Arkham Asylum Breakout, Jokerland
SET NUMBERS: 6860, 10937, 76035
YEARS: 2012, 2013, 2015

Leaves curl through Ivy's flaming red hair.

A kiss from these sly lips will soon make you snooze.

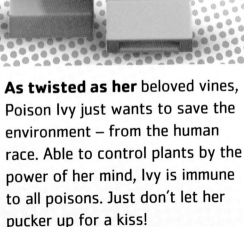

Poison Ivy's leafy costume is also printed on the back.

THE ECO-WARRIOR
The 2006 Poison Ivy minifigure had exclusive dark red hair, green lips and black eyes with light green eye shadow. Although a brilliant botanist, she would still love to escape her greenhouse-styled prison in Arkham Asylum (set 7785).

As twisted as her beloved vines, Poison Ivy just wants to save the environment – from the human race. Able to control plants by the power of her mind, Ivy is immune to all poisons. Just don't let her pucker up for a kiss!

THE SCARECROW
MASTER OF FEAR

VITAL STATS
....

LIKES: Striking fear into the hearts of everyone
DISLIKES: Bullies
FRIENDS: The Arkham Asylum inmates
FOES: Batman and Robin
SKILLS: Escape bids
GEAR: Scarecrow hat

SET NAME: Batman: Arkham Asylum Breakout
SET NUMBER: 10937
YEAR: 2013

Wide-brimmed scarecrow hat

Scary cloth face

Rope fashion accessories

His tattered clothing is also printed on the back of the minifigure.

LIVING NIGHTMARE

Luckily, Scarecrow doesn't have Nyctophobia, fear of the dark, or Cleithrophobia, fear of being locked up, as he spends lots of time in jail. Not that it would matter, as his earlier 2006 minifigure, in set 7786, had a glow-in-the-dark head!

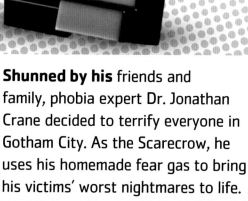

Shunned by his friends and family, phobia expert Dr. Jonathan Crane decided to terrify everyone in Gotham City. As the Scarecrow, he uses his homemade fear gas to bring his victims' worst nightmares to life.

SCARECROW'S BIPLANE
AS THE CROW FLIES

Scarecrow holds
onto his scythe
while flying

Biplanes take
their name from
having two sets
of wings.

Scary scarecrow
face on tail fin

GREEN FEAR
GAS BOMBS

As well as having
two tanks of fear
gas ready to spray, Scarecrow's
Biplane is also equipped with
fear gas bombs. Coloured the
same ghastly green, they have
horrible grinning pumpkin
heads inside!

Spinning
propeller

One of four
machine guns

Scarecrow scythes through the sky
in his biplane. It might look old-
fashioned, but its four machine guns
are very high-tech: perfectly placed
to fire between moving rotor blades.
Plus it carries weapons that are the
cutting-edge of criminal chemistry!

THE RIDDLER
GOTHAM CITY'S CLUED-UP CRIMINAL

VITAL STATS

LIKES: Dangling sidekicks from cranes
DISLIKES: Straight talking
FRIENDS: The Joker, Harley Quinn
FOES: Batman and Robin
SKILLS: Creating riddles
GEAR: Question-mark cane

SET NAMES: The Dynamic Duo Funhouse Escape
SET NUMBERS: 6857
YEARS: 2012

DID YOU KNOW?
The Dynamic Duo Funhouse Escape set includes a mini-Riddler mannequin in the ticket office.

The 2012 Riddler minifigure now wears a bowler hat in place of black hair.

Defined muscles show through green suit

There's no question about the Riddler's favourite punctuation mark!

CARRIED AWAY
In 2006, the Riddler was carted off to Arkham Asylum (set 7785) sporting a shock of black hair and a slightly simpler green outfit. This variant also cropped up in The Bat-Tank: The Riddler and Bane's Hideout (set 7787).

One of Gotham City's most confusing villains, Edward Nygma likes to leave a trail of cryptic clues to help Batman foil his crimes. No one knows why. It's a complete mystery, and the most puzzling of all of the Riddler's riddles.

HARLEY QUINN
DIAMOND DEVIANT

VITAL STATS
....

LIKES: Rollercoasters
DISLIKES: Heroic characters
FRIENDS: The Joker,
the Riddler
FOES: Batman and Robin
SKILLS: Setting traps
GEAR: Rollercoaster car

SET NAMES: The Dynamic
Duo Funhouse Escape
SET NUMBERS: 6857
YEARS: 2012

A revolving head
reveals a
mischievous grin.

Harley Quinn was the
first LEGO minifigure
to wear a jester's hat.

ARMED TO THE TEETH
The 2008 Harley Quinn from set
7886 had a wide, manic grin,
but had not yet learnt good
dental care – her teeth were
stained a horrible yellow colour!
Mocking her looks, however,
is not advised, as she's equipped
with not one, but two, weapons!

The red and black
card game colour
scheme continues
with diamond motifs.

Harleen Quinzel was the Joker's
doctor at Arkham Asylum, but
instead of curing her criminal
patient, she joined him on a crazy
crime spree as Harley Quinn. Now,
she has fun causing chaos in Gotham
City with her beloved puddin' Mr J!

HARLEY'S HAMMER TRUCK
MANIC MOTOR

Harley's minifigure holds yet another hammer.

"WHACK-A-BAT" scrawled on hammer

HAMMER TIME

Batman rides a winged Batcycle in pursuit of Harley's Hammer Truck. Both his armour and the motorcycle have the same flat-topped bat-symbol up front.

Monster-truck wheels

Look out: Harley Quinn is hitting the streets – literally! Her mashing machine has a huge mechanical hammer to whack anything in its path. Batman had better move fast to stop her giving his Batcycle a flat tyre – and a flat everything else!

BANE
BRAWN AND BRAINS COMBINED

Head encased in a mask so Bane can constantly breathe in Venom

Artificially developed muscles

No gloves: Bane likes to break things with his bare hands

THREE-WHEELING

Similar in dress apart from his blue trousers and slightly different head mask, the 2007 Bane still looks tough and brutish. He patrols his hideout in set 7787 on a three-wheeled dirt bike equipped with a missile launcher and a sidecar with a laser weapon.

Don't be fooled by all those muscles, super-villain Bane is no meathead. Able to speak dozens of different languages, this menacing mastermind uses a serum known as Venom to give himself super-strength and agility.

THE JOKER
STILL THINKS HE'S FUNNY

VITAL STATS

LIKES: A good laugh
DISLIKES: Arkham Asylum
FRIENDS: Harley Quinn
FOES: Batman and Robin
SKILLS: Chemistry
GEAR: Remote control

SET NAMES: Dynamic Duo's Funhouse Escape, Batwing Battle over Gotham City, Batman: Defend the Batcave, The Joker Bumper Car
SET NUMBERS: 6857, 6863, 10672, 30303
YEARS: 2012, 2014, 2015

Yellow teeth revealed in wide grin on one side of head

New waistcoat design features a lurid lime-green pattern

BEHIND THE SMILE

The Joker's manic laughter hides a keen intelligence. His fiendish plots are full of surprises, which is why a spin of this minifigure's head reveals a sneaky smirk.

Remote control for Joker's latest barmy bat-trap!

Still mad, bad and dangerous to know, the Joker is up to his same old tricks. With a yellow grin stretched across the chalk-white face of this minifigure variant, Batman's greatest enemy is about to launch his own brand of toxic laughing gas.

BANE'S DRILL TANK
UNDERWORLD UNDERMINER

VITAL STATS

OWNER: Bane
USED FOR: Underground attacks
GEAR: Missile launchers, giant drill

SET NAMES: The Batcave
SET NUMBERS: 6860
YEARS: 2012

Lamp lights dark tunnels

Rotating drill carves through rock and earth

Missile ready to launch

BIKE STRIKEBACK

Inside the Batcave, Batman uses his Batcycle to take on Bane's Drill Tank. It is similar to the Batcycle in The Dynamic Duo Funhouse Escape (set 6857), but has yellow wheels and missile launchers.

Six wheels turn the caterpillar tracks

With its tunnel-boring machinery at the front, Bane's Drill Tank is primed to mine its way into the Batcave for a surprise attack on Batman and Robin! The armoured front also puts an impressive amount of space between the driver and his nemesis.

THE JOKER'S HENCHMAN
NO CLOWNING AROUND

VITAL STATS

LIKES: Being a grump
DISLIKES: Smiling
FRIENDS: The Joker
FOES: Batman
SKILLS: Helicopter pilot
GEAR: Laughing gas bomb

SET NAME: Batwing Battle Over Gotham City
SET NUMBER: 6863
YEAR: 2012

This henchman never fancies turning his frown upside down!

Lime green to match the Joker's vest

Black gloves leave no fingerprints

BACK TO BASICS

There's no mistaking who this moaning minifigure works for. Not only are his clothes the Joker's trademark colours, but the Clown Prince of Crime's face is emblazoned on his back.

The Joker's henchman likes to crack safes but not smiles. This misery-guts is never happy. Maybe he doesn't like having his face painted. He'd better watch out, just in case the Joker gives him a dose of all that laughing gas!

THE JOKER'S HELICOPTER
TAKING A FUNNY TURN

DID YOU KNOW?
Set 6863 is an update of The Batwing: The Joker's Aerial Assault (set 7782) from 2006.

"J" is for Joker

Toxic laughing-gas bomb

HA-HA-HANG ON!
The Joker loves to show off, and can't help swinging on a rope ladder with a joke-shop gun while his henchman is left with the serious job of controlling the chopper.

Launchers for missiles – one on each side

Uncharacteristically, there are big grins all round the Joker's Helicopter. Both sides show the Joker's own sinister smile, while the bomb at the front has a fearsome leer. Needless to say, it's filled with laughing gas!

TWO-FACE
A MAN DIVIDED

Scarred
face

Dynamite is
ready to blow

The original
2006 Two-Face
minifigure used
a LEGO stud
as a coin, but
this variant has
a printed
round tile.

Two-Face's
split-colour
suit continues
on the back of
his minifigure.

MAKING HIS MIND UP

Two-Face made a bad decision
when he stole a safe from
Gotham City museum. Batman
pursued and made sure the
villain was soon laughing on
the other side of his face.

Talk about double-trouble.
Former District Attorney Harvey
Dent still plans his crimes on the flip
of his two-headed coin. This updated
variant adds crazy colour to his
originally black and white wardrobe.

Project Editor Emma Grange
Editors Tina Jindal, Matt Jones, Ellie Barton,
Clare Millar, Rosie Peet
Senior Designers Nathan Martin, Mark Penfound,
David McDonald
Designers Karan Chaudhary, Stefan Georgiou
Pre-Production Producer Kavita Varma
Senior Producer Lloyd Robertson
Managing Editors Paula Regan,
Chitra Subramanyam
Design Managers Neha Ahuja, Guy Harvey
Creative Manager Sarah Harland
Art Director Lisa Lanzarini
Publisher Julie Ferris
Publishing Director Simon Beecroft
Additional Photography Markos Chouris,
Christopher Chouris, Gary Ombler

First published in Great Britain in 2016
by Dorling Kindersley Limited
80 Strand, London, WC2R 0RL

001–298875–Jul/16

Contains content previously published in LEGO® DC COMICS
SUPER HEROES *Character Encyclopedia* (2016)

Page design copyright © 2016 Dorling Kindersley Limited
A Penguin Random House Company

A CIP catalogue record for this book
is available from the British Library.

ISBN: 978-0-2412-9286-0

Printed and bound in China

www.LEGO.com
www.dk.com

A WORLD OF IDEAS:
SEE ALL THERE IS TO KNOW

ACKNOWLEDGMENTS
ACKNOWLEDGEMENTS

DK would like to thank Randi Sørensen,
Paul Hansford, Martin Leighton Lindhardt, Maria
Bloksgaard Markussen, Adam Corbally, Daniel
Mckenna, Casper Glahder, Adam Siegmund Grabowski,
John Cuppage, Justin Ramsden, Karl Oskar Jonas
Norlen, Marcos Bessa, Sally Aston, Sven Robin Kahl
and Mauricio Bedolla at the LEGO Group; Ben Harper,
Thomas Zellers and Melanie Swartz at Warner Bros.;
Cavan Scott and Simon Hugo for their writing;
Katie Bowden for editorial assistance and Sam
Bartlett for design assistance.